Rhythm In Motion

VOLUME 1: EXPLORING THE ART

RINI ALOYSIA JOHN

INDIA · SINGAPORE · MALAYSIA

ISBN 979-8-89475-600-4

Rhythm In Motion

VOLUME 1: EXPLORING THE ART

Contents

About The Author

Rini John, a seasoned professional boasting over a decade of extensive experience as Head of Performing Arts and Specialist Teacher. With a diverse skill set encompassing Performing Arts, Drama, Music & Movement, and Dance, Rini brings a wealth of expertise to her craft.

Rini's journey is a testament to her unwavering dedication and remarkable achievements in the field. From choreographing competitions and musical productions to spearheading notable events, her proficiency in choreography, event management, and academic excellence shines through.

At the core of Rini's approach lies a profound commitment to preparing students for success, both academically and artistically. Her ability to curate comprehensive dance curricula tailored to meet the diverse needs of her students reflects her profound technical understanding and subject matter expertise.

In every aspect of her career, Rini John remains steadfast in her pursuit of excellence. With a boundless passion for dance and an unwavering commitment to student success, she continues to make a profound impact in the realms of performing arts education and beyond. Join Rini on this transformative journey into the world of dance education and unlock your full potential as a dancer and artist.

Introduction

"Rhythm in Motion: Exploring the Art " is a captivating and comprehensive book that delves into the enchanting world of dance, providing an insightful and inspiring exploration of this timeless art form. From its rich history to its diverse genres and transformative power, this book celebrates the beauty and significance of dance in our lives.

Drawing upon extensive research and personal experiences, the author takes readers on a mesmerizing journey, unraveling the origins of dance and tracing its evolution throughout different cultures and eras. Through vivid descriptions and engaging anecdotes, the book brings to life the vibrant tapestry of dance, showcasing its role as a universal language that transcends boundaries and connects people across time and space.

"Rhythm in Motion" series of book delves into the various dance forms, from classical ballet to contemporary, jazz to Latin, and everything in between.

Each chapter explores the unique characteristics, techniques, and expressive qualities of these genres, providing valuable insights for dancers and enthusiasts alike. With interviews and profiles of renowned dancers and choreographers, the book offers a glimpse into the lives and creative processes of these artists, inspiring readers to embrace their own passion for dance.

The book also dives into the significance of dance as a means of personal expression and emotional release. It explores the transformative power of movement, delving into how dance can heal, empower, and transform individuals physically, emotionally, and mentally. Through captivating stories and personal anecdotes, readers are encouraged to embrace dance as a form of self-discovery and self-expression, regardless of age, background, or skill level.

In addition, "Rhythm in Motion" provides practical advice and guidance for aspiring dancers, offering tips on technique, training, and performance preparation. It covers essential topics such as body conditioning, injury prevention, and the importance of discipline and perseverance, equipping readers with the tools they need to embark on their own dance journeys.

Above all, "Rhythm in Motion: Exploring the Art of Dance" serves as a celebration of the joy, beauty, and transformative power of dance. Whether you're an avid dancer, a curious enthusiast, or simply someone who appreciates the artistry of movement, this book is a must-read, inspiring readers to embrace the rhythm of life through the magic of dance.

Chapter 1: The Universal Language of Dance Through Time

The pounding beats of ancient drums reverberate as bodies sway to primal rhythms. This is the genesis of dance, a kinetic language that transcends words and speaks directly to our spirit. In this first chapter, we travel back in time to uncover dance's origins and significance.

For millennia, dance has facilitated human expression. From ancient ceremonial rites to joyous celebrations, dance is woven into the cultural fabric of civilizations worldwide. By exploring artifacts, texts, and traditions, we will trace dance's evolution and adaptation across diverse eras and regions.

Dance constantly transforms, shaped by the cultural shifts of each age. We will embark on a captivating journey through dance history, from its ancestral roots in ritual to revolutionary modern incarnations. Join us as we follow the footsteps of dancers through the ages, revealed as innovators and chroniclers of our shared humanity through movement. Together we will discover dance's enduring power to transform and connect.

PRIMITIVE MOVEMENTS AND RITUALS:

Before spoken language, early humans communicated through gestures and rhythmic motions. Tribal dances and ceremonial rites allowed people to express emotions, share messages, and bond. Through stomping, clapping, and swaying, these primal dances fostered unity with each other and the natural world.

THE SACRED AND MYTHOLOGICAL:

Across cultures worldwide, dance has long conveyed myths and spiritual beliefs. We explore ancient sacred dances from Africa's masked rituals to Greece's ecstatic Dionysian rites. Dance served as a storytelling vessel, bringing legends vividly to life while connecting people to deities and the cosmos.

INDIA: DEVOTION EMBODIED IN DANCE

Indian dance forms like Bharatanatyam and Odissi originated in Hindu temples, expressing devotion through movement. Dancers use precise footwork, hand gestures, and facial expressions to depict gods and goddesses, imparting myths and invoking spiritual connections. These graceful dances continue to transport audiences into mystical realms today.

BHARATANATYAM: GRACE AND DEVOTION

With Tamil Nadu roots, Bharatanatyam's intricate motions and Hindu tales demonstrate deep spirituality. Dancers embody Lord Shiva and others, sharing divine stories. Beyond entertainment, Bharatanatyam evokes devotion in performers and spectators through each careful gesture and pose.

ODISSI: ELEGANCE AND EMOTION

In Odisha, Odissi's fluid grace narrates myths through sculpture-like poses and emotional expressiveness. Depicting tales like the Mahabharata, Odissi explores love, devotion and more through delicate hand gestures and body contours. Odissi beautifully embodies India's mythical ethos.

KATHAKALI: THEATRICAL SPLENDOR

Hailing from Kerala, Kathakali blends dance, music and elaborate artistry to convey epics. Intense training shapes the intricate footwork, faces and eye acting that bring gods to life. Vivid costumes, makeup and gestures tell Ramayana tales in an amplified, theatrical manner that fully immerses audiences.

MANIPURI: DIVINE GRACE AND SERENITY:

Originating from the northeastern state of Manipur in India, Manipuri dance reflects the region's unique cultural heritage and spiritual traditions. It is deeply rooted in Vaishnavism, a form of Hinduism dedicated to Lord Vishnu and his incarnations, particularly Lord Krishna. Manipuri dancers, often adorned in vibrant traditional costumes, portray stories from the life of Lord Krishna and the Radha-Krishna love legends. The dance form emphasizes graceful and gentle movements, reflecting the serene and devotional nature of Manipuri spirituality. With its circular motions, delicate footwork, and emotive expressions, Manipuri dance transports the audience into a realm of divine love, devotion, and transcendence.

KATHAK: EMOTION OF LOVE:

Kathak dancers skillfully depict a wide range of mythological characters and stories, adding a spiritual dimension to their performances. Through their movements, gestures, and expressions, dancers embody the essence and emotions of these revered figures, captivating the audience with their portrayals.

Lord Krishna and Radha: The love story between Lord Krishna and Radha is a recurring theme in Kathak dance. Dancers evoke the playful and tender moments shared between the divine couple, conveying their deep love and devotion through intricate footwork, expressive facial expressions, and graceful hand gestures. The tales of Krishna's mischievous pranks, his enchanting flute melodies, and Radha's eternal longing are brought to life through the nuanced storytelling of Kathak.

The mythological dances of India, with their intricate movements, expressive storytelling, and spiritual depth, are a testament to the country's rich cultural heritage. Through the medium of dance, ancient mythologies come alive, captivating audiences and connecting them to the realms of gods, goddesses, and epic tales.

GREECE: EPICS AND ECSTASY:

In ancient Greece, dance played a significant role in religious ceremonies and celebrations. The Dionysian rites, dedicated to the god of wine and fertility, involved ecstatic dances that sought to connect with the divine and evoke altered states of consciousness. Through these frenzied and wild movements, participants sought to experience a union with the divine, transcending the boundaries of the physical world. Greek mythology also inspired narrative dances, such as the tragic tale of Orpheus and Eurydice, which were performed to honor the gods and communicate moral lessons.

Chapter 2
Indigenous Dance Cultures Across the Globe

From ancient times, indigenous communities worldwide have used dance as a powerful medium to express their cultural identity, spiritual beliefs, and connection to the natural world. These dance traditions, deeply rooted in ancestral wisdom, serve as a bridge between the past and the present, preserving the rich heritage and diversity of indigenous peoples.

- **Africa:** Embodying Ancestral Spirits The African continent is home to a multitude of indigenous dance cultures, each reflecting the unique customs, beliefs, and histories of its diverse ethnic groups. From the energetic movements of the Maasai people in East Africa to the mesmerizing, masked dances of the Dogon tribe in West Africa, these dances invoke a deep sense of community, spirituality, and cultural pride. Vibrant costumes, intricate footwork, and rhythmic music come together to celebrate nature, commemorate important milestones, and honor ancestral spirits. These dances embody the wisdom passed down through generations, fostering a strong connection to the land and the ancestors.

- **Australia:** Dreamtime Connections Indigenous Australians have preserved their rich cultural heritage through a wide range of dance traditions. In Aboriginal cultures, dance serves as a means of storytelling, passing down ancient narratives known as Dreamtime stories. These dances depict creation stories, totems, and ancestral connections to the land, embodying a deep reverence for the natural world. From the graceful movements of the Yolngu people in the north to the energetic dances of the Torres Strait Islanders in the east, indigenous Australian dances foster a strong connection between past, present, and future generations.

- **North America:** Sacred Rituals and Powwows Indigenous dance cultures in North America represent various tribal nations and their unique traditions. Powwows, vibrant social gatherings, often showcase traditional dances such as the Fancy Dance, Jingle Dance, and Grass Dance. Accompanied by rhythmic drumming and singing, these dances celebrate community, honor ancestors, and preserve cultural heritage. Each dance style carries specific meanings and symbolic elements, reflecting the spiritual beliefs and stories of indigenous peoples, fostering a sense of unity and cultural resurgence.

- **South America:** Ancestral Wisdom in Motion South America is home to a multitude of indigenous cultures, each with distinct dance traditions deeply intertwined with spiritual beliefs and cultural practices. From the vibrant costumes and rhythmic movements of the Quechua people in the Andes to the ancestral rituals of the Amazonian tribes, indigenous dances serve as a conduit for connecting with nature, honoring deities, and invoking ancestral wisdom. These dances often embody elements of the natural world, such as animals, plants, and celestial bodies, bridging the human and spiritual realms.

- **Balinese Rituals:** A Harmonious Offering On the island of Bali, Indonesia, dance is an integral part of religious rituals and ceremonies. Balinese dance, often accompanied by gamelan music, offers a captivating blend of intricate movements, expressive gestures, and vibrant costumes. Dances such as the Legong and Barong tell mythological tales of battles between good and evil forces, invoking blessings and protecting the community. The dances are seen as a form of spiritual offering to the gods, with performers meticulously trained in their art form, ensuring the preservation of ancient traditions and spiritual connections.

Sacred mythological dances found worldwide are a testament to the enduring power of movement to convey spiritual stories, connect with the divine, and preserve cultural heritage. From Africa to Bali, from India to Greece, these dances bridge the gap between the seen and the unseen, inviting us to explore the mysteries of the human experience. As we witness the profound expressions of devotion, storytelling, and spiritual connection in these dances, we gain a deeper appreciation for the universal language of movement and its ability to transcend cultural boundaries, reminding us of our shared humanity and the enduring legacy of ancient mythologies.

Chapter 3: Rituals and Ceremonies: Exploring the Sacred Dimensions of Movement

Throughout history, dance has played a significant role in rituals and ceremonies, serving as a profound medium for spiritual expression, communal celebration, and transformative experiences. Across diverse cultures and traditions, dance has been used to honor deities, mark significant life events, invoke blessings, and connect with the divine. In this chapter, we delve into the captivating world of rituals and ceremonies in dance, exploring their cultural significance, symbolism, and the transformative power they hold.

Ritual dance is deeply embedded in cultures worldwide, serving as a means to communicate with the spiritual realm, honor ancestors, and uphold cultural traditions. These dances often reflect the values, beliefs, and historical narratives of communities, transmitting cultural knowledge from one generation to the next. Whether performed in sacred spaces, during seasonal festivals, or as part of life-cycle events, ritual dance serves as a communal expression of identity, spirituality, and social cohesion.

SYMBOLISM AND SACRED GESTURES:

Ritual dances are often infused with symbolic gestures and movements that carry profound meaning within their cultural context. These gestures, known as mudras or specific choreographic patterns, convey metaphysical concepts, depict mythological narratives, or invoke divine qualities. For example, in Indian classical dance, mudras represent various elements of nature, deities, emotions, and cosmic forces. Similarly, Indigenous dances may incorporate animal imitations, elemental movements, or ceremonial attire to symbolize connections with the natural world and ancestral spirits.

TRANSCENDENCE AND TRANSFORMATION:

Ritual dance holds the potential to transport participants and observers beyond the ordinary realm, facilitating a sense of transcendence and spiritual connection. The repetitive movements, rhythmic patterns, and communal engagement create a collective energy that heightens the spiritual experience. Dance becomes a transformative process, allowing individuals to enter a state of altered consciousness, catharsis, or union with the divine. Through rhythmic ecstasy, participants often find liberation, healing, and a deepened sense of belonging to something greater than themselves.

CEREMONIAL DANCE IN LIFE EVENTS:

Dance plays a central role in various life events, marking significant transitions and honoring important milestones. Weddings, coming-of-age ceremonies, birth celebrations, and funerals often incorporate ceremonial dances that symbolize the journey of individuals or communities. These dances serve as expressions of joy, grief, unity, and the continuity of traditions. They strengthen social bonds, invoke blessings, and create a collective memory that shapes the cultural fabric of societies.

CONTEMPORARY EXPRESSIONS OF RITUAL DANCE:

While traditional ritual dances continue to be practiced, contemporary expressions of ritualistic movement have also emerged. Artists and choreographers draw inspiration from ancient traditions, infusing them with modern interpretations and aesthetics. These contemporary ritual dances explore themes of identity, spirituality, and social justice, using movement as a vehicle for personal and collective transformation.

Rituals and ceremonies in dance embody the sacred dimensions of human existence. They connect us to our cultural roots, foster spiritual connections, and provide transformative experiences. Whether performed in sacred spaces, cultural gatherings, or personal rites of passage, ritual dance is a testament to the enduring power of movement as a means of spiritual expression, cultural preservation, and communal celebration. By embracing and honoring these rituals, we recognize the profound significance of dance in shaping our individual and collective narratives.

As human societies developed, dance became intimately intertwined with rituals and ceremonies, marking significant moments in the lives of individuals and communities. Through the lens of anthropology and archaeology, we unravel the symbolism embedded within these rituals, revealing dance as a bridge between the physical and spiritual realms, a conduit for transcendent experiences.

As we conclude this exploration of primitive movements and rituals, we recognize dance as an innate human language, capable of transcending cultural barriers and connecting individuals across time and space. From the rhythmic gestures of early humans to the sacred dances of ancient civilizations, dance has served as a profound means of expression, celebration, and spiritual connection. In the following chapters, we will further unravel the diverse genres and styles of dance, tracing their evolution and discovering the myriad ways in which movement continues to captivate our bodies, minds, and souls. So let us step forward, embracing the ancient rhythms and dances that have shaped our collective human journey.

Chapter 4: Courtly Elegance and Renaissance Dance: Reviving Grace and Refinement

A cultural rebirth swept Europe during the Renaissance, sparking curiosity, creativity, and refinement in courtly life. Dance became central, serving as a symbol of nobility through elegance, grace, and status. This chapter explores Renaissance court dances, from intricate steps to lavish costumes, unveiling their beauty and cultural impact.

THE COURTLY IDEAL: ELEGANCE AND ETIQUETTE

In the fancy courts long ago, dance showed elegance, grace, and good manners. The Courtly Ideal style of dance was popular in the Renaissance and Baroque. It showed the nobility's fine taste and proper behaviour.

This article looks at what the Courtly Ideal dance was about. It focused on elegance and etiquette. The stylish movements and polite conduct left a lasting effect on dance.

ETIQUETTE AND PROTOCOL: THE DANCE OF SOCIAL ORDER

The Courtly Ideal Dance was not just about fancy moves. It also showed the court's social order and proper manners. On the dance floor, each bow, curtsy, and gesture followed strict rules of etiquette. These movements showed the dancers' status and respect for each other. The protocols mirrored the court's hierarchy and customs.

Dance masters polished the Courtly Ideal style. They trained the courtiers in graceful technique and polite conduct. The masters taught excellent posture, footwork, and body positions. But they also stressed good etiquette between dance partners. This upheld values like respect and self-control. The dance masters helped make the dances refined displays of etiquette and elegance.

DANCE SUITES AND CREATIVE MOVES

Courtly Ideal dances were often done as suites - a series of dances in a row. These suites showed off the dancers' skill and artistry. They flowed through different tempos, styles, and moods.

Each dance in the suite had its own flavour and creative moves. This lets dancers showcase their technique while sticking to elegance. They could interpret the music their way, with spins, leaps, and steps suited to each dance. But they always maintained the Ideal of grace and manners. The suites displayed the dancers' versatility within the refined Courtly style.

LASTING IMPACT OF COURTLY DANCE

The Courtly Ideal style had a big influence on later dance. Its focus on grace, proper technique, and etiquette shaped many dance forms. For example, it impacted ballet and the court dances of future eras. The ideals of elegance and manners from the Courtly dance still affect dance today. They set standards for good etiquette and respect between dance partners. And they keep inspiring the cultivation of refined artistry.

Courtly dances have a long history in cultures worldwide. They were performed in royal courts, noble homes, and aristocratic circles. While the specific dances varied, they shared qualities of elegance, grace, and finesse.

BALLET DE COUR (FRANCE)

Ballet de Cour originated in the French royal courts during the Renaissance. This early ballet form combined lavish costumes, music, poetry, and elegant choreography. Ballet de Cour laid the foundations of classical ballet as we know it today.

The term "Ballet de Cour" means "court ballet" in English. These performances were tied to the opulent lifestyles of the French aristocracy. Kings Louis XIV and Louis XV used the Ballet de Cour as royal entertainment and artistic expression.

Ballet de Cour productions were grand spectacles with intricate dance sequences, music, storytelling, and elaborate sets. The choreography focused on courtly etiquette, graceful posture, and refined technique. This distinguished Ballet de Cour from other dance forms.
Steps included pliés, relevés, jumps, and precise arm gestures. Bows and curtsies reflected courtly manners. Composer Jean-Baptiste Lully and choreographer Pierre Beauchamp collaborated on influential productions.

While originating among French nobility, Ballet de Cour evolved into more theatrical forms. However, its emphasis on refinement and etiquette continues to shape ballet traditions today.

ALLEMANDE (GERMANY)

The Allemande was a graceful Renaissance and Baroque court dance from Germany. Performed at social gatherings and in royal courts, couples glided through elegant footwork and partnering. The Allemande embodied courtly sophistication and etiquette ideals.
The term "Allemande" comes from French, meaning "German" - denoting

its origins. Danced to instrumental music in triple meter, couples moved in a line exchanging gestures and turns. The steps intertwined gracefully through movements like the pas de bourrée and balancé.

Intricate hand-holds like crossed hands and half-turns were signature. The Allemande influenced later Baroque and Classical era dances. While the style faded by the 1800s, its elegance remains appreciated in dance history today.

JAPANESE COURT DANCES

Japanese Court Dances like Kagura and Bugaku have an ancient lineage intertwined with imperial culture. Combining stylized movements, lavish costumes, and symbolic gestures, they embody the elegance of Japan's royal courts.

Kagura means "god-entertainment" in Japanese. These dances honoured Shinto gods through music and movement. Kagura began in ancient times when people thought dances pleased the gods. They hoped this would bless the imperial court and nation.

Kagura dances feature flowing steps, poses, and gentle gestures. Traditional Japanese instruments like drums and flutes provide music. Bugaku originated from 7th-century continental influences. Its refined choreography was reserved for nobility. Meticulous gestures and footwork require rigorous training.

The stunning costumes feature vibrant colours, patterns, and lavish fabrics denoting social status. Props and masks add drama and symbolism.

Passed down through generations, these dances preserve imperial culture. Though once exclusive to nobility, they now promote public appreciation of this graceful artistry.

Bugaku means "elegant music" in Japanese. These dances came from China and Korea in the 600s. Bugaku was very refined, only for emperors and nobles. The dances combined court etiquette, music, and graceful moves. Performers trained rigorously to master the complex steps and gestures.

Both Kagura and Bugaku value detail. Each subtle gesture and foot position has a symbolic meaning. The dances tell stories, events, or natural wonders, expressing deep culture.

The costumes are elaborate, with intricate patterns and rich fabrics. They show the dancers' status and enhance their grace. Masks, fans, and props add drama.

These court dances preserve culture through generations. Specific styles are kept for rituals and festivals. Now some are open to the public, showcasing this graceful art.

The beauty of these dances reflects Japan's heritage. They honour the refinement of imperial courts. Preserving court dances upholds traditions and spirituality.

PAVANE (SPAIN)

The Pavane is a slow and fancy dance that started in Spain during the Renaissance. It became popular all over Europe and was an important dance in the Spanish and English royal courts. The Pavane is known for its slow and dignified movements, beautiful costumes, and rich musical accompaniment. It was a symbol of how refined and sophisticated the royal courts were.

The word "Pavane" comes from the Spanish word "pavana," which means "peacock." This name fits well because the dance tries to look like the graceful movements and regal presence of a peacock. The Pavane was often performed at formal events like weddings, coronations, and big processions, to show off elegance and courtly spectacle.

The Pavane is known for its slow tempo and deliberate, gliding steps. Dancers move in a procession, usually in pairs or small groups, with their arms held gracefully and their bodies upright. The steps include smooth, flowing movements like walking steps, side steps, and turns. The dance is often done in a measured and synchronized way, creating a visually striking group.

The Pavane is accompanied by live music, played on instruments like lutes, violins, and other period-specific instruments. The music is melodic and harmonious, adding to the grandeur and emotional impact of the dance. The rhythm of the music sets the pace for the dancers, guiding their movements with poise and grace.

The costumes worn during the Pavane were very fancy and beautiful. This showed the wealth and fashion of the Renaissance period. Dancers wore fine fabrics, and dresses with embroidery, jewellery, feathers, and other fancy accessories. The costumes added to the visual excitement of the dance. They made the sense of courtly elegance and grandeur even stronger.

The Pavane had a big influence on the development of dance and music during the Renaissance. It inspired composers to create musical pieces specifically for the dance, like the famous "Pavane in F-sharp minor" by Gabriel Fauré. The dance also influenced other courtly dances, including the Galliard, which was often performed as a lively contrast to the slow Pavane.

Over time, the Pavane changed and adapted in different regions of Europe. In England, it became the "Pavan," which had a slightly faster tempo and more complicated footwork. In Spain, the dance continued in different forms, changing based on regional styles and influences. Although the Pavane became less popular in later centuries, its legacy remains as a symbol of courtly elegance and refined dance. Today, the Pavane is sometimes performed at events recreating historical dances, period-themed events, and by early music groups.

The Pavane shows the rich cultural heritage of Spain and its contributions to the art of dance. Its slow, graceful movements and regal demeanour continue to fascinate audiences, giving a glimpse into the courtly traditions and refined aesthetics of the Renaissance era.

MINUET (FRANCE AND ENGLAND)

The Minuet is a fancy and refined dance from royal courts. It started in France in the 1600s and later became popular in England. The Minuet is one of the most well-known dances from the Baroque period. It is known for its graceful and precise movements, complicated footwork, and elaborate costumes. These things showed the elegance and sophistication of royal courts at that time.

At first, the Minuet was danced at social events in French royal courts and among nobles. Later, it spread to the English court and became an important part of formal events and balls. The name "Minuet" comes from the French word "menu," which means "small." This refers to the small steps and gentle motions done by the dancers.

The Minuet is a couples' dance, traditionally done by pairs facing each other. The dancers move in a series of measured steps, taking small deliberate strides, often with graceful hand gestures and little bows. The footwork includes specific steps like the pas de Menuet, balancé (a rocking step), and coupé (a cutting step). The dance is known for its smooth, flowing movements done with poise and precision.

The Minuet is usually danced to music in triple meter, with a moderate tempo. Composers like Jean-Baptiste Lully and Johann Sebastian Bach composed minuets specifically for dance performances. The melodies and rhythms perfectly matched the dance's structure and style.

The costumes worn for Minuet performances were very fancy and fashionable, reflecting the trends of the Baroque period. Men wore tailored suits, often decorated with lace and ornate trims, while women wore luxurious gowns with intricate embroidery and embellishments. The costumes enhanced the visual appeal of the dance and also showed the social status and refinement of the dancers.

The Minuet became popular across Europe during the 1700s and was even danced in colonial America. It was considered a high-status dance and was featured prominently in royal court settings, royal balls, and social gatherings. As the dance became more popular, variations and regional styles emerged, incorporating local influences and preferences.

The Minuet had a lasting impact on the development of dance and music. Its elegant movements and refined footwork influenced the evolution of other courtly dances, such as the Gavotte and the Quadrille. The structure and rhythm of the Minuet also influenced musical compositions, with composers integrating the dance form into orchestral suites, operas, and instrumental pieces.

Despite becoming less popular in the 1800s, the Minuet has remained a representation of the courtly elegance and social grace of the Baroque era. Today, it is still occasionally performed at events recreating historical dances, period-themed events, and by Baroque music groups.

The Minuet stands for the rich cultural heritage of France and England, showcasing the refined aesthetics, social customs, and artistic sensibilities of the Baroque period. Its graceful movements and elegant demeanour continue to fascinate and captivate audiences, offering a glimpse into the sophisticated world of courtly dance and music.

THE GAVOTTE COURT DANCE (FRANCE)

The Gavotte is a lively and elegant court dance that originated in France during the 16th century. It gained popularity throughout Europe and became one of the most beloved dances of the Baroque period. The Gavotte is known for its spirited and rhythmic movements, intricate footwork, and joyful expression, making it a staple of courtly entertainment and social gatherings.

The Gavotte takes its name from the French folk dance called "gavot," which originated in the province of Gavot in southeastern France. Over time, the dance evolved into a refined courtly dance that was embraced by nobility and aristocracy. The Gavotte is characterized by its moderate tempo, typically performed in quadruple meter and its distinctive rhythmic pattern.

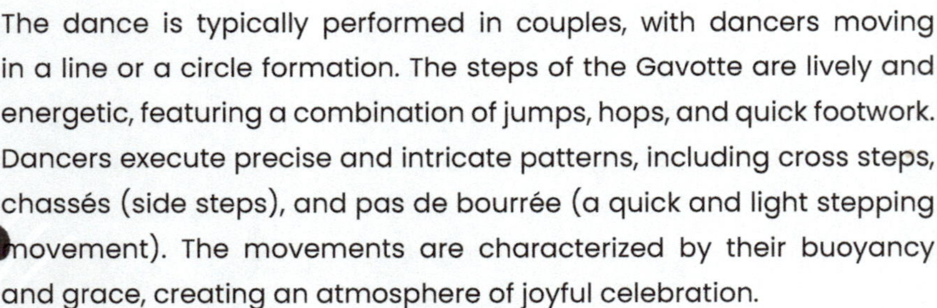

The dance is typically performed in couples, with dancers moving in a line or a circle formation. The steps of the Gavotte are lively and energetic, featuring a combination of jumps, hops, and quick footwork. Dancers execute precise and intricate patterns, including cross steps, chassés (side steps), and pas de bourrée (a quick and light stepping movement). The movements are characterized by their buoyancy and grace, creating an atmosphere of joyful celebration.

The music accompanying the Gavotte is often composed in binary form, consisting of two sections, each repeated. It is typically played by a chamber ensemble, featuring instruments such as violins, flutes, and harpsichords. The melodies are lively and spirited, reflecting the energetic nature of the dance. The music provides a rhythmic structure and serves as a guide for the dancers' movements.

The Gavotte was not only performed at royal court events but also became a popular dance at social gatherings, balls, and celebrations. It was often featured in theatre performances and ballets, adding a touch of elegance and joy to the entertainment at that time. As the dance grew more popular, variations and regional styles emerged, incorporating local influences and preferences.

The Gavotte had a significant impact on the development of dance and music during the Baroque period. It influenced composers to include Gavotte movements in their compositions, such as the orchestral suites of Johann Sebastian Bach. The dance form also influenced the evolution of other courtly dances, including the Minuet and the Quadrille.

Although the Gavotte became less popular in the 1700s, it continued to be appreciated as a nostalgic dance from the past. It was revived during the 1800s and 1900s as part of events recreating historical dances, period-themed events, and by Baroque music groups.

The Gavotte shows the rich cultural heritage of France and its contributions to the world of dance. Its lively movements and joyful spirit capture the essence of courtly celebration and social interaction during the Baroque period. The dance continues to delight audiences with its infectious rhythm and graceful choreography, offering a glimpse into the elegance and charm of a bygone era.

BALINESE COURT DANCES (INDONESIA)

Balinese Court Dances, also known as "Tari Bedaya" or "Tari Pendet," are a vibrant and sacred dance form that originated in the royal courts of Bali, Indonesia. These courtly dances are an integral part of Balinese culture and are deeply rooted in religious rituals and artistic traditions. With their intricate movements, elaborate costumes, and mesmerizing music, Balinese Court Dances showcase the rich heritage and spiritual essence of the island.

Balinese Court Dances are performed to honour the deities and ancestors, as well as to entertain and bless the royal court and the community. These dances are often associated with temple ceremonies, royal processions, and important social events. The dancers, usually female, are highly skilled and trained from a young age to embody grace, precision, and spirituality in their movements.

One of the most iconic Balinese Court Dances is the "Pendet Dance." It is performed as a welcoming dance, marking the beginning of ceremonies or special events. The dancers

carry small trays adorned with flowers, rice, and incense, which they sprinkle as offerings to invite the deities and purify the space. The Pendet Dance is characterized by delicate hand movements, gentle steps, and serene facial expressions.

Another prominent Balinese Court Dance is the "Legong Dance." It is a narrative dance that depicts traditional Balinese stories and mythology. The Legong Dance is performed by young girls who undergo rigorous training to master the intricate footwork, hand gestures, and intricate eye movements. Accompanied by a gamelan orchestra, the dancers tell stories of love, bravery, and divine encounters through their movements and expressions.

The costumes worn in Balinese Court Dances are very fancy and ornately decorated, reflecting the cultural and artistic traditions of Bali. The dancers wear bright, handwoven fabrics, intricately decorated headdresses, and elaborate jewellery. The costumes are designed to enhance the beauty and elegance of the dancers, while also conveying the symbolic meaning of the dance and its story.

Music plays a vital role, with the hypnotic sounds of the gamelan orchestra accompanying the dancers' movements. The gamelan ensemble consists of various percussion and melodic instruments, such as gongs, drums, xylophones, and metallophones. The complex rhythms and melodies add depth and intensity to the performances, creating a mesmerizing experience for both dancers and the audience. Balinese Court Dances not only express art but also carry deep spiritual and cultural significance. They are believed to bring blessings, harmony, and protection to the community. The dances are passed down through generations, with masters and teachers ensuring the preservation of the dance forms and their sacred rituals.

In recent years, these dances have gained international recognition and are often showcased in cultural festivals worldwide. They serve as ambassadors of Balinese culture, captivating audiences with their beauty, grace, and spiritual resonance.

The enduring legacy lies in their ability to transport viewers into a world of mythology, spirituality, and artistic expression. They embody Bali's rich heritage, reflecting the island's devotion to tradition, beauty, and spiritual connection. Through their performances, Balinese Court Dances continue to celebrate the profound beauty and sacredness of Balinese culture.

THAI COURT DANCES

Thai Court Dances, also known as "Khon," are a captivating and intricate dance form that originated in the royal courts of Thailand. Rooted in tradition and steeped in cultural significance, Thai Court Dances showcase the grace, elegance, and artistry of the Thai people.

Thai Court Dances are highly stylized and incorporate elements of drama, music, and storytelling. They are often performed as part of royal ceremonies, celebrations, and special events. These dances have deep connections to Thai mythology, history, and religious beliefs, making them an essential part of the country's cultural identity.

One of the most prominent Thai Court Dances is the "Khon Masked Dance." It features performers wearing ornate masks, elaborate costumes, and intricate headpieces. The dancers skillfully execute choreographed movements, combining graceful gestures, precise footwork, and acrobatic techniques. The Khon Masked Dance reenacts episodes from the Ramakien, the Thai adaptation of the Indian epic, the Ramayana, depicting stories of gods, heroes, and mythical creatures. Another notable Thai Court Dance is the "Fawn Thai Dance," also known as the "Classical Thai Dance." This dance form emphasizes the graceful movements of the female dancers, characterized by delicate hand gestures, flowing arm movements, and precise footwork. The Fawn Thai Dance often tells stories from Thai folklore, literature, and history, showcasing the cultural heritage and artistic finesse of the Thai people.

Thai Court Dances are accompanied by traditional Thai music, which includes a variety of instruments such as the ranat ek (a xylophone-like instrument), the pi phat (a set of gongs), and the khong wong lek (a small brass percussion instrument). The melodic and rhythmic patterns of the music enhance the emotional impact of the dance, creating a harmonious blend of sight and sound.

The costumes worn in Thai Court Dances are very elaborate and intricately designed. They are made from luxurious fabrics, adorned with gold and silver thread, and decorated with shimmering gemstones and intricate embroidery. The costumes vary depending on the specific dance and character being portrayed, with each design representing the social status, mythology, or historical context of the performance.

Thai Court Dances require extensive training and discipline to master. Dancers undergo years of rigorous practice to perfect their techniques, maintain proper posture, and convey the emotions and stories of the dances. The dances are often passed down through families or taught in traditional dance schools, ensuring the preservation and continuation of this important cultural art form.

Thai Court Dances have not only played an important role in Thai royal courts but have also become renowned internationally. They are frequently showcased in cultural festivals, theatre performances, and dance competitions around the world, serving as a window into Thailand's rich cultural heritage and captivating audiences with their beauty and artistry.

Through their movements, elaborate costumes, and enchanting storytelling, Thai Court Dances transport viewers into a world of mythical beings, historical legends, and cultural traditions. They reflect the deep spirituality, artistic excellence, and cultural pride of the Thai people, preserving and celebrating the nation's heritage for generations to come.

These are just a few examples of courtly dances from different cultures. Each dance form carries its unique cultural significance and reflects the elegance and sophistication of royal court life in various regions around the world.

The Courtly Ideal Dance stood as a pinnacle of elegance, grace, and social etiquette in the courts of the past. It represented the epitome of refined manners, showcasing the artistry and sophistication of the nobility. By embodying the Courtly Ideal Dance, dancers not only expressed their physical abilities but also demonstrated their understanding and mastery of social decorum. Though its heyday has passed, the Courtly Ideal Dance's influence and legacy continue to resonate, reminding us of its timeless beauty.

FOLK AND TRADITIONAL DANCES: HEARTBEATS OF CULTURE

The stomping of feet, the swaying of colourful skirts, the clapping of hands - these are the heartbeats that give life to folk and traditional dances around the world. From lively Irish jigs to graceful Japanese fan dance, these dance forms carry the stories, customs, and identities of communities.

Chapter 5: The Global Influence of Dance

Dance has a powerful way of bringing people together across the world. As cultures have mixed and exchanged ideas, many new and exciting dance styles have been created. This section explores how dance styles have spread and fused across continents.

From the energetic Afro-Cuban rhythms of salsa to the vibrant hip-hop moves born on the streets of New York City, we see how sharing cultures can create something new and amazing. The stories of pioneering artists and the emergence of unique dance styles show the resilience and adaptability of dance as it continues to evolve in our rapidly changing world.

Picture dancers in a salsa club in Havana, Cuba. The lively Latin rhythms fill the air as couples twirl and step. But salsa didn't start in Cuba - it was created when the musical traditions of Africa, Spain, and the Caribbean collided together in a wonderful fusion. The energy and passion of salsa bring together influences from multiple continents.

In the lively neighbourhoods of New York City, a new dance style emerged in the 1970s. Called hip-hop, it was born from the creativity and expression of young people from diverse backgrounds. Set to a beat of funk, soul, and synthesized rhythms, hip-hop dancers developed intricate footwork, dynamic freezes, and acrobatic moves that reflected the urban environment around them. What started on the streets soon spread to become a globally recognized dance form.

These are just two examples of how dance has the incredible power to bridge cultures. When people share traditions and are open to new influences, truly magical things can happen. From classic ballet being reimagined with modern flair, to traditional folk dances incorporating contemporary moves, the global influence of dance shows that artistic expression knows no borders.

So let's celebrate the pioneering dancers, choreographers and communities who have embraced cultural exchange. It is through the fusion of styles that dance continues to evolve and connect people across the globe. As the world grows smaller through technology and travel, we can look forward to even more exciting new dance forms emerging on the world stage.

Imagine the green hills of Ireland, where laughter fills the misty air as dancers kick up their heels in a joyful jig. The lively fiddle music pushes them forward, their steps beating a rhythmic sound against the earth, like a thousand pounding hearts. Here, the dance celebrates strength, showing the indomitable spirit of people who have overcome both hardships and triumphs.

In the cherry blossom-lined streets of Japan, the gentle fluttering of fans adds a mesmerizing layer to the graceful movements of the Nihon Buyo dancers. With each precise gesture and elegant turn, they evoke the timeless beauty of nature. The delicate petals drifting on the wind are mirrored in the swaying of their colourful kimonos. This dance honours tradition, connecting the present to the past and providing a sense of cultural continuity.

Picture the lively Mexican folk dances, where the vibrant skirts of the dancers twirl and swish, their movements as exciting as the mariachi music that accompanies them. In the rhythmic clapping and infectious energy, you can feel the spirit of community, the bonds formed through shared joy and celebration. Here, the dance symbolizes togetherness, showing the power of unity.

From the lively steps of the Ghoomar dance in India, where dancers move in synchronized circles, to the intricate footwork of Flamenco in Spain, where passion and intensity ignite every move, folk and traditional dances are the heartbeats that connect us to the rich tapestry of human culture. Through these dances, we experience the stories, struggles, triumphs, and enduring spirit of diverse communities worldwide.

Conclusion

As we conclude this first chapter of "Rhythm in Motion: Exploring the Art of Dance," we stand in awe of the ancient roots and universal language of dance. From its humble beginnings as a primal instinct to its multifaceted expressions in contemporary society, dance remains an integral part of human culture. In the chapters to come, we will dive deeper into the various dance genres, exploring their techniques, emotions, and transformative power. So, let us take the next step together on this extraordinary journey through the rhythm and motion of dance.

Notes

Notes

Notes

Notes

Notes

www.ingramcontent.com/pod-product-compliance
Lightning Source LLC
Chambersburg PA
CBHW040916110726

48005CB00006B/916